Pebble® Plus

Animal Group Behavior

by Abbie Dunne

CAPSTONE PRESS
a capstone imprint

Pebble Plus is published by Capstone Press,
1710 Roe Crest Drive, North Mankato, Minnesota 56003
www.capstonepub.com

Copyright © 2017 by Capstone Press, a Capstone imprint. All rights reserved. No part of this publication may be reproduced in whole or in part, or stored in a retrieval system, or transmitted in any form or by any means, electronic, mechanical, photocopying, recording, or otherwise, without written permission of the publisher.

Library of Congress Cataloging-in-Publication Data
Names: Dunne, Abbie, author.
Title: Animal group behaviors / by Abbie Dunne.
Description: North Mankato, Minnesota : Capstone Press, [2017] | Series:
   Pebble plus. Life science | Audience: Ages 4-8.? | Audience: K to grade
   3.? | Includes bibliographical references and index.
Identifiers: LCCN 2016005323| ISBN 9781515709442 (library binding) | ISBN
   9781515709763 (pbk.) | ISBN 9781515711117 (ebook pdf)
Subjects: LCSH: Social behavior in animals--Juvenile literature. | Animal
   behavior--Juvenile literature.
Classification: LCC QL775 .D86 2017 | DDC 591.56--dc23
LC record available at http://lccn.loc.gov/2016005323

Editorial Credits
Linda Staniford, editor; Bobbie Nuytten, designer; Jo Miller, media researcher;
Tori Abraham, production specialist

Photo Credits
Capstone Studio: Karon Dubke, 21; Newscom: Minden Pictures/Ingo Arndt, 11; Shutterstock: Alan Jeffery, 13, bikeriderlondon, 7, JONATHAN PLEDGER, 9, Matt9122, 15, Miao Liao, 19, Rich Carey, cover, Shamleen, 17, Stubblefield Photography, 5, timsimages, 1

Design Elements
Shutterstock: Alena P

Note to Parents and Teachers

The Life Science set supports national curriculum standards for science. This book introduces the concept of animal group behavior. The images support early readers in understanding the text. The repetition of words and phrases helps early readers in understanding the text. This book also introduces early readers to subject-specific vocabulary words, which are defined in the Glossary section. Early readers may need assistance to read some words and to use the Table of Contents, Glossary, Read More, Internet Sites, Critical Thinking Using the Common Core, and Index sections of the book.

Printed in the United States   5061

Table of Contents

What Is Group Behavior?

Some animals live in groups. Living in groups helps them to survive. Animals in a group protect each other. They look for food together too.

Protecting Each Other

Penguins live in huge groups
called colonies. They huddle
together to keep warm. Birds
on the edge of the group
look out for predators.

Elephant mothers and babies live in herds. The mothers help protect the babies. Living in a group helps the elephants survive.

Gorillas live in small family groups called troops. The biggest male protects all of the gorillas in the troop.

Hunting and Eating

Wolves live in small groups called packs. The pack hunts together. A single wolf cannot catch big animals. But the pack can! All of the wolves get more food.

Dolphins live in groups in the ocean. Together they hunt for fish. The dolphins surround the fish and catch them.

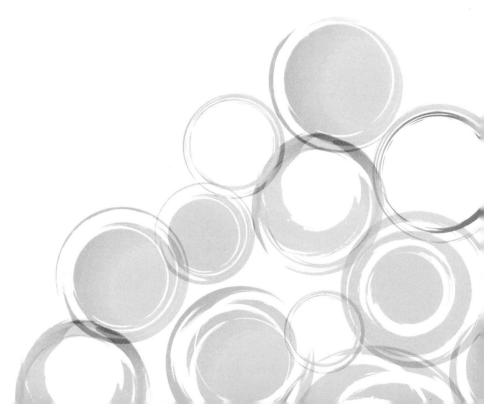

Working Together

Ants live in groups called colonies.

Each ant in a colony has a job.

Some take care of baby ants.

Others find food for the colony.

Sharing work helps the ants survive.

Migration

Some animals migrate
in winter. Flocks of birds
fly south to find food
and warmer places to live.

Activity

Do people and animals have similar group behaviors? Find out!

What You Need

- pencil
- 5 index cards
- crayons

What You Do

1. Write "Herd" on one index card. Ask an adult to help you find out more information about animals that live in herds, such as elephants. Write two facts about animal herds on that card.

2. On the back of the index card, draw a picture of people acting as a herd.

3. Write "People Herd" on the back of the index card. Write why you think the people acted as a herd.

4. Write "Pack" on the second index card. Repeat steps 1–3 for animals that live in packs.

5. Do the same for School, Colony, and Migrate on the rest of the index cards.

What Do You Think?

Make a claim.

A claim is something you believe to be true.

Do people act in groups like other animals? Use facts from your cards.

Herd
- The mothers in an Elephant
- Elephants walk in a single fil

Glossary

colony—large group of insects or other animals that live together

flock—group of the same kind of animal; members of a flock live, travel, and eat together

migrate—to move from one place to another

predator—an animal that hunts other animals for food

protect—to guard or keep safe from harm

school—a large number of the same kind of fish swimming and feeding together

surround—enclose on all sides

survive—to stay alive

troop—a large group

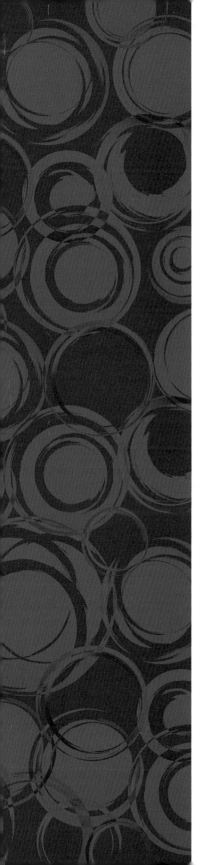

Read More

Kuskowski, Alex. *A School of Fish: Animal Groups in the Ocean.* Minneapolis, Minn.: ABDO, 2013.

Tjernagel, Kelsi Turner. *Animals that Live in Groups.* Learn about Animal Behavior. Mankato, Minn.: Capstone Press, 2013.

Wright, Anna. *A Tower of Giraffes: Animals in Groups.* Watertown, Mass.: Charlesbridge, 2015.

Internet Sites

FactHound offers a safe, fun way to find Internet sites related to this book. All of the sites on FactHound have been researched by our staff.

Here's all you do:

Visit *www.facthound.com*

Type in this code: 9781515709442

 Super-cool stuff! Check out projects, games and lots more at **www.capstonekids.com**

Critical Thinking
Using the Common Core

1. Some animals and birds migrate in the winter. Why do you think they do this? (Key Ideas and Details)

2. What is a group of wolves called? (Key Ideas and Details)

3. How do you think living in a group helps wolves survive? (Integration of Knowledge and Ideas)

4. Ants live in colonies. Can you think of other insects that live in colonies? (Integration of Knowledge and Ideas)

Index